Paul's Three Ministries

By Michael Penny

ISBN: 978-1-78364-330-1

www.obt.org.uk

THE OPEN BIBLE TRUST
Fordland Mount, Upper Basildon,
Reading, RG8 8LU, UK

www.obt.org.uk

Paul's Three Ministries

Contents

A TRIBUTE TO PAUL

One good reason why Christianity was triumphant was that it found in Saul of Tarsus, later St. Paul, a missionary of genius. What he preached had little to do with the historic Jesus, a preacher of a very different kind. His concern, so fierce and deep that he gave himself no rest, was with the resurrected Christ, the Saviour-God, the Redeemer, who was revealed in that vision on the road to Damascus. A guilty man crying to other guilty men, in a world doomed to be stricken with sin and death, he preached salvation through Christ. He must have blazed through that pagan twilight like a rocket.

Though himself a Jew, Paul took this new and startling religion, as far removed from perfunctory offerings to Fortune as a cry of "Fire!" is from a bid at bridge, out of Judaism into the world of the Gentiles.

J.B. Priestly, Man and Time page 156.

1.

Introduction

1. INTRODUCTION

Acts chapter seven records Stephen's long speech before the Jewish Sanhedrin and when he had concluded they were furious. Undeterred he carried on and said, "I see heaven open and the Son of Man standing at the right hand of God." At this they rushed at him, dragged him out of the city and began to stone him. Those who had witnessed against Stephen laid their clothes at the feet of a *young man* named Saul who approved of this execution, (Acts 7:56; 8:1). Almost insignificantly a new character is introduced onto the pages of Scripture. Who is this Saul? We are not told but as we continue reading we find that from that day onwards, great persecution broke out against the church at Jerusalem and all, except the apostles, were scattered throughout Judea and Samaria. Who was behind such oppression? It was Saul, amongst others, who began to destroy the church. Going from house to house, he dragged off both men and women and put them in prison, (Acts 8:1-3).

As most of the Christians fled from Jerusalem Saul soon found he had few to persecute but he was intent on this action. Breathing out murderous threats against the Lord's disciples he went to the high priest and asked for letters to the synagogues in Damascus, so that if he found any Christians there, whether men or women, he might take them prisoner to Jerusalem, (Acts 9:1-2). No doubt the high priest eagerly agreed and Paul set off for Damascus but: -

> As he neared Damascus on his journey, suddenly a light from heaven flashed around him. He fell to the ground and heard a voice say to him, "Saul, Saul, why do you persecute me?" "Who are you, Lord?" Saul

asked. "I am Jesus, whom you are persecuting," he replied. "Now get up and go into the city, and you will be told what you must do." The men travelling with Saul stood there speechless; they heard the sound but did not see anyone. Saul got up from the ground, but when he opened his eyes he could see nothing. So they led him by the hand into Damascus. For three days he was blind, and did not eat or drink anything. (Acts 9:3-9)

In Damascus there was a disciple called Ananias. The Lord called to him in a vision, "Ananias!" "Yes, Lord," he answered. The Lord told him, "Go to the house of Judas on Straight Street and ask for a man from Tarsus named Saul, for he is praying. In a vision he has seen a man named Ananias come and place his hands on him to restore his sight." "Lord," Ananias answered, "I have heard many reports about this man and all the harm he has done to your saints in Jerusalem. And he has come here with authority from the chief priests to arrest all who call on your name." But the Lord said to Ananias, "Go! This man is my chosen instrument to *carry my name before the Gentiles and their kings and before the people of Israel.* I will show him how much he must suffer for my name." Then Ananias went to the house and entered it. Placing his hands on Saul, he said, "Brother Saul, the Lord – Jesus, who appeared to you on the road as you were coming here – has sent me so that you may see again and be filled with the Holy Spirit." Immediately, something like scales fell from Saul's eyes, and he could see again. He got up and was baptised, and after taking some food, he regained his strength. (Acts 9:10-19)

This Saul was now a changed man and, as often happened to people in the Scriptures, he had his name changed, to Paul, (Acts 13:9). But who was he? Where did he come from? We can find out more about him from his own words. Before the crowd at Jerusalem he said:

> I am a Jew, born in Tarsus of Cilicia, but brought up in this city. Under Gamaliel I was thoroughly trained in the law of our fathers and was just as zealous for God as any of you are today. I persecuted followers of this Way to their death, arresting both men and women and throwing them into prison, as also the high priest and all the council can testify. (Acts 22:3-5)

When writing to the Philippians, Paul described himself as having been:

> Circumcised on the eighth day, of the people of Israel, of the tribe of Benjamin, a Hebrew of the Hebrews; in regard to the , a Pharisee; as for zeal, persecuting the church; as for legalistic righteousness, faultless. (Philippians 3:5-6)

Thus Saul, who became Paul, was a Pharisee, so keen to preserve all he believed that he persecuted the Christian church. He hounded its followers out of Jerusalem and followed them to Damascus but he never got there as Saul, The Pharisaic Jew. He arrived there as Paul, the blinded Christian. What was the Lord doing in using a man like Paul, who had consented to the stoning of Stephen and who had imprisoned Christian men and women?

That this was an important event in the plan of God can be seen from the fact that Saul's conversion is recorded no fewer than three times in the Scriptures. With the exception of the ministry and work of the Lord Jesus Christ, few other events are recorded twice, let alone three times. But with Saul's conversion to Paul, the Holy Spirit saw fit to have it written down in Acts 9, 22 and 26. (See page 6.)

Not only did Paul meet his Savior on the Damascus Road but he was also commissioned. The Lord told Ananias that "this man is my chosen instrument to carry my name **before the Gentiles** and their kings and **before the people of Israel**," (Acts 9:15). Thus right from the start there appears to be a duality to Paul's ministry. He was to carry the Lord's name to two very different groups of people; the Gentiles and the people of Israel. But what was he to say to them? Would his message be the same for each? Such a two-fold ministry would not be easy as one group had been brought up on the Law of Moses with its signs and symbols, its types and shadows, its commandments and regulation. The other had its roots in paganism with influences from the Greeks and their mystery cults.

In the account of his conversion in Acts 22, Paul was told by Ananias that he was to be the Lord's witness "to *all* men of what you have seen and heard," (verse 15). But what had he seen and heard up to this point? We may now know exactly, but it is clear from Scripture that Paul was to learn much more after that time. In the third account of the Damascus Road experience we read that the Lord had said to Paul:

I have appeared to you to appoint you as a servant and as a witness of what you have seen of me and what I will show you. (Acts 26:16)

What *had* Paul seen? What was he to be *shown?* The only way we can answer these questions is to go back and see what Paul said and did in his life.

ACTS 9:3-19

As Paul neared Damascus on his journey, suddenly a light from heaven flashed around him. He fell to the ground and heard a voice say to him, "Saul, Saul, why do you persecute me? "Who are you, Lord?" Saul asked. "I am Jesus whom you are persecuting," he replied. "Now get up and go into the city, and you will be told what you must do."

Saul got up from the ground, but when he opened his eyes he could see nothing. So they led him by the hand into Damascus. For three days he was blind, and did not eat or drink anything.

In Damascus there was a disciple named Ananias. The Lord called to him in a vision, "Ananias!" "Yes Lord," he answered. The Lord told him, "Go to the house of Judas on Straight Street and ask for a man from Tarsus named Saul, for he is praying. In a vision he has seen a man named Ananias come and place his hands on him to restore his sight."

"Lord," Ananias answered, I have heard many reports about this man and all the harm he has done to your saints in Jerusalem. And he has come here with authority from the chief priests to arrest all who call on your name."

But the Lord said to Ananias, "Go! This man is my chosen instrument to carry my name before the Gentiles and their kings and before the people of Israel."

ACTS 22:6-21

About noon as I came near Damascus, suddenly a bright light from heaven flashed around me. I fell to the ground and heard a voice say to me, "Saul! Saul! Why do you persecute me?" Who are you Lord?" I asked. "I am Jesus of Nazareth, whom you are persecuting," he replied …

"What shall I do Lord?" I asked. Get up," the Lord said, "and go into Damascus. There you will be told all that you have been assigned to do."

My companions led me by the hand into Damascus, because the brilliance of the light blinded me.

A man named Ananias came to see me. He was a devout observer of the law and highly respected by all the Jews living there. He stood beside me and said, "Brother Saul, receive your sight!" And at that very moment I was able to see again.

Then he said: "The god of our fathers has chosen you to know his will and to see the Righteous one and to hear words from his mouth. You will be his witness to all men of what you have seen and heard. And now what are you waiting for? Get up, be baptised and wash your sins away, calling on his name."…

The Lord said to me, "Go; *I will send you far away to the Gentiles.*"

ACTS 26:12-22

On one of these journeys I was going to Damascus with the authority and commission of the chief priests. About noon, O king, as I was on the road, I saw a light from heaven, brighter than the sun, blazing around me and my companions. We all fell to the ground, and I heard a voice saying to me in Aramaic, "Saul, Saul, why do you persecute me? It is hard for you to kick against the goads."

Then I asked, "Who are you Lord?" I am Jesus, whom you are persecuting," the Lord replied. "Now get up on your feet. I have appeared to you to appoint you as a servant and as a witness of what you have seen of me and what I will show you. I will rescue you from your own people and from the Gentiles. I am sending you to open their eyes and turn them from darkness to light, and from the power of Satan to God, so that they may receive forgiveness of sins and a place among those who are sanctified by faith in me."

So then, King Agrippa, I was not disobedient to the vision from heaven. First to *those in Damascus, then to those in Jerusalem and Judea, and to the Gentiles also,* I preached that they should repent and turn to God and prove their repentance by their deeds.

2.

What you have seen

2. WHAT YOU HAVE SEEN

After being blinded on the Damascus Road, Paul was led into the city and for three days he neither ate nor drank. Then Ananias went to him and healed him and baptised him. Paul spent several days with the disciples in Damascus.

> At once he began to preach in the synagogues that *Jesus is the Son of God*. All those who heard him were astonished…Yet Saul grew more and more powerful and baffled the Jews living in Damascus by proving that *Jesus is the Christ* (Messiah). (Acts 9:20-22)

This was the first thing Paul did. He preached that the One who had appeared to him on the Damascus Road was the Son of God. He proclaimed that this crucified, resurrected and ascended Jesus of Nazareth was the Messiah (Christ). This was what Paul *had* seen and he witnessed to it straightaway. As such his message was in complete harmony with that of the twelve apostles, including John, who wrote his gospel for this very reason. He said these signs "are written that you may believe that Jesus is the Christ, the Son of God, and that by believing you may have life in his name," (John 20:31).

Paul so baffled the Jews at Damascus that they conspired to kill him, but he escaped. Eventually Paul arrived in Jerusalem where he stayed with the Christians who had returned to the city and he moved freely about, speaking boldly in the name of the Lord. He talked and debated with the Greek-speaking Jews about Jesus, but one can only deduce that they were baffled and could not answer him for they tried to kill him also. Paul was taken to Caesarea and then sent to his hometown of Tarsus, (Acts 9:23,28-30). We hear no more about this man for a while but eventually Barnabas went to Tarsus to look for Paul and when he found him, he brought him to Antioch. There, for a whole year, these two met with the church and taught a great number of people. Eventually they were dispatched to Jerusalem bearing gifts for the Christians living in Judea, (Acts 11:25-26,30).

Evidently, they returned from Jerusalem for in Acts 13:1 they were both back in Antioch where the Holy Spirit gave out some special instructions:

> "Set apart for me Barnabas and Saul for the work which I have called them." So after they had fasted and prayed, they placed their hands on them and sent them off. The two of them sent on their way by the Holy Spirit, went down to Seleucia and sailed from there to Cyprus. When they arrived at Salamis, they proclaimed the word of God in the Jewish synagogues. (Acts 13:2-5)

What they proclaimed in these synagogues can be seen from the first major speech of Paul, recorded in Acts 13:16-41. This address is based squarely on the Old Testament, demonstrating that Jesus of Nazareth is the One spoken about in the Scriptures and the One Who fulfilled them. The central point is again that this *Jesus is the Son of God,* (Acts 13:33). The recurrent theme that runs through Paul's ministry in Acts is that Jesus is the resurrected One, the Son of God, the Christ (Messiah). For example:

(1) At Damascus "Saul grew more and more powerful and baffled the Jews living in Damascus by proving that Jesus is the Christ." (Acts 9:22)

(2) At Pisidian Antioch Paul preached, "We tell you the good news: What God promised our fathers he has fulfilled for us, their children, by raising up Jesus. As it is written in the second Psalm: 'You are my Son; today I have become your Father." (Acts 13:32, 33)

(3) At Thessalonica "he reasoned with them from the Scriptures. Explaining and proving that the Christ had to suffer and rise from the dead. 'This Jesus I am proclaiming to you is the Christ,' he said." (Acts 17:2, 3)

(4) At Corinth "Paul devoted himself exclusively to preaching, testifying to the Jews that Jesus was the Christ." (Acts 18:5)

(5) Paul taught Priscilla and Aquila who taught Apollos and "he (Apollos) vigorously refuted the Jews in public debate, proving from the Scriptures that Jesus was the Christ." (Acts 18:28)

(6) At Jerusalem Paul recounted his Damascus Road experience stating that the voice from heaven was Jesus of Nazareth. (Acts 22:8)

(7) Before Agrippa Paul again stated that the voice was Jesus and that "the Christ would suffer." (Acts 26:15,23)

(8) At Rome Paul tried to convince the leaders of the Jews "about Jesus from the Law of Moses and from the Prophets." (Acts 28:27, 23)

There can be little doubt that what Paul had already seen was the great truth that Jesus of Nazareth was the Christ (Messiah). He was the Son of God. There may well have been other things that Paul had seen but this great truth dominated his ministry from that time. Straightaway he preached this at Damascus and continued to do so throughout his ministry.

3.

What I will show you

3. WHAT I WILL SHOW YOU

There are also four references to the Son of God in Galatians (1:16; 2:20; 4:4,6) and this epistle may help us in our quest to find out what Paul was taught later. However, in the first chapter Paul sets about defending the gospel saying that "even if we or an angel from heaven should preach a gospel other than the one we preach to you, let him be eternally condemned," (Galatians 1:8). Paul's character had not changed. He was still as zealous as ever but now it was not for Pharisaic legalism but for the gospel of grace. The former originated with men, but the latter?

> I want you to know, brothers, that the gospel I preached is not something that man made up. I did not receive it from any man, nor was I taught it; rather I received it by revelation from Jesus Christ. (Galatians 1:11,12)

Paul follows this defence with a brief account of his life and focuses on the early years following his conversion.

> But when God, who set me apart from birth and called me by his grace, was pleased to reveal his Son in me so that I might preach him among the Gentiles, I did not consult with any man, nor did I go up to Jerusalem to see those who were apostles before I was, but I went immediately into Arabia and later returned to Damascus. Then after three years, I went up to

Jerusalem to get acquainted with Peter and stayed with him fifteen days. (Galatians 1:15-18)

Here Paul spoke about a time in Arabia when, possibly, the Lord fulfilled "What I will show you" but that time did not exhaust the revelations for we read that fourteen years later "I went up again *in response to a revelation* and set before them the Gospel that I preach among the Gentiles," (Galatians 2:1,2). Thus this gospel was precious to Paul for he had received it directly from the Lord Jesus Christ, by revelation. In case there is any doubt about the contents of this gospel, it is, perhaps, wise to quote Paul himself.

> Now, brothers, I want to remind you of the gospel I preached to you, which you received and on which you have taken your stand. By this gospel you are saved, if you hold firmly to the word I preached to you. Otherwise you have believed in vain. For what I received I passed on to you as of first importance: that Christ died for our sins according to the Scriptures, that he was buried, that he was raised on the third day according to the Scriptures. (1 Corinthians 15:1-4).

From Paul's first major speech at Pisidian Antioch we can see that this gospel had an important place in what he said.

> But the one whom God raised from the dead did not see decay. Therefore, my brothers, I want you to know that through Jesus the forgiveness of sins is proclaimed to you. Through him everyone who believes is justified from everything you could not be justified from by the Law of Moses. (Acts 13:36-39)

This gospel of righteousness/justification through faith/belief in Christ is another major part of Paul's preaching. Certainly the message that the righteous shall live by faith could be called Paul's hallmark, (Romans 1:17; Galatians 3:11; Hebrews 10:28).

4.
Paul's
First and
Second
Ministries

4. PAUL'S FIRST AND SECOND MINISTRIES

When we read through the Acts of the Apostles we see that Paul was commissioned by the Holy Spirit in Acts 13:2-4. This resulted in him proclaiming the word of God in the Jewish synagogue at Salamis. After this he went to Pisidian Antioch and, on the Sabbath day, entered the synagogue of the Jews and sat down, but they invited Paul to speak and he stood up and addressed the congregation, (Acts 13:5,14,16). This was to be the pattern of Paul's activities everywhere he went.

At Iconium Paul and Barnabas went, as usual to the Jewish synagogue, (Acts 14:1). When they came to Thessalonica there was a Jewish synagogue and Paul, as his custom was, went in and on three Sabbath days reasoned with them from the Scriptures, explaining and proving that Christ had to suffer and rise from the dead, (Acts 17:1-3). At Berea, they went to the Jewish synagogue, (Acts 17:10). At Athens Paul reasoned in the synagogues with the Jews, (Acts 17:16,17). At Corinth, every Sabbath day he reasoned in the synagogue, trying to persuade the Jews, (Acts 18:4). At Ephesus Paul entered the synagogue and spoke boldly for three months, arguing persuasively about the kingdom of God, (Acts 19:8). Three days after arriving in Rome, Paul called together the leaders of the Jews, (Acts 28:17).

There can be no doubt about it that this man had a ministry to the people of Israel, in line with what the Lord had said to Ananias: "This man is my chosen instrument to carry my name before the Gentiles and their kings and *before the people of Israel,"* (Acts

9:15). Everywhere he went he addressed the people of Israel first. Even in his epistle to the Romans he stated clearly that this people had the first place and certain advantages.

> I am not ashamed of the gospel, because it is the power of God for the salvation of everyone who believes: first for the Jew, then for the Gentile. (Romans 1:16) There will be trouble and distress for every human being who does evil: first for the Jew, then for Gentile; but glory, honour and peace for everyone who does good: first for the Jew, then for the Gentile. (Romans 2:9,10) What advantage, then is there in being a Jew, or what value is there in circumcision? Much in every way! First of all, they have been entrusted with the very words of God. (Romans 3:1-2)

Here, under the inspiration of the Holy Spirit, Paul was stating that Israel had the first place and this is reflected in his ministry throughout the book of Acts. However, some people object to this view because of the following verses where Paul is called

- The apostle to the Gentiles. (Romans 11:13)
- A minister of Jesus Christ to the Gentiles. (Romans 15:16)
- The prisoner of Jesus Christ for you Gentiles. (Ephesians 3:1)

Some read the above verses to mean that Paul's ministry was exclusively to and for Gentiles but such a reading cannot be correct. A simple reading of Acts shows that everywhere Paul went he sought out the synagogue of the Jews and spoke to them first about the Lord Jesus Christ. Also the Lord's words in Acts 9:15, "This man is my chosen instrument to carry my name before the Gentiles and their kings and *before the people of Israel,"* clearly indicate that Paul had been given a ministry to Israel. Why, then, is his name so linked with the Gentiles? An answer may lie in the word *ethnos,* which is translated Gentiles but which means, simply, nations. Depending on the context *ethnos* may mean all nations including Israel or all nations excluding Israel. Only the context can decide which is best. Certainly, Paul had a message to both Israel and the other nations, of that there can be no doubt.

Another passage which must be considered in the light of the present discussion is Galatians 2:6-9.

> As for those who seemed important – whatever they were makes no difference to me; God does not judge by external appearance – those men added nothing to my message. On the contrary, they saw that I had been given the task of preaching the gospel to the Gentiles (*ethnos*), just as Peter had been given the task of preaching the gospel to the Jews For God, who was at work in the ministry of Peter as an apostle to the Jews. For God, who was at work in the ministry of Peter as an apostle to the Jews, was also at work in my ministry as an apostle to the Gentiles (*ethnos*). James, Peter and John, those reputed to be pillars, gave me and Barnabas the right hand of fellowship when they recognized the grace given to me. They agreed that we should go to the Gentiles (*ethnos*), and they to the Jews.

In view of this last sentence some may be perplexed as to why Paul continued to go to the Jews throughout his tours of the Mediterranean world. The answer may again lie in this word *ethnos.* It has been suggested that the agreement was that Peter, James, John and company were to minister to Israel *in the land* but that Paul Barnabas and company were to witness to the nations outside of the land, and that would include the dispersion of Israel. However, both James and Peter wrote epistles for the dispersion. It may be that Paul was particularly linked with the Gentiles simply because he was given special additional ministry to them which was different from that of the twelve, with whom he shared a ministry to the people of Israel. This is certainly what happened and we find that during this period Paul had two ministries; one to the dispersion of Israel and one to the Gentiles. Was there any significant difference between these two ministries? No and Yes!

No with respect to the person of the Lord Jesus. He was the Son of God, the Christ, the promised Messiah. No, with respect to the message of sins being forgiven and righteousness accredited by believing in the Lord Jesus Christ. With respect to sin and salvation, there was neither Jew nor Greek, (Galatians 3:28). However, when we carefully consider the Acts of the Apostles and the epistles written during that time, we will see that there were considerable differences on non-fundamental issues. What was said of or asked from the Christian Jews could be quite different from what was said of or asked from the Christian Gentiles. We shall need to consider these, but to do so we shall need to put them in their context and have some idea about God's overall plan for the people of Israel and the Gentile nations.

5.

God's Plan for Israel and the Nations

5. GOD'S PLAN FOR ISRAEL AND THE NATIONS

At the end of Genesis 11 Abram, whose name was later changed to Abraham, comes onto the scene. He was given certain unconditional promises by God. He was told he would have a land, that he would be the father of a great nation through which all peoples of the earth were to be blessed, (Genesis 12:1-3). This land was promised to him and his offspring, and its borders were the river of Egypt and the Euphrates, (Genesis 13:14-17;15:16). Similar promises were made to Isaac and Jacob, (Genesis 26:24; 28:13,14), but none of these three patriarchs, the fathers of the nation of Israel, nor any of their offspring have inherited this land in full and the promise can be fulfilled only in resurrection. This was the hope of the people of Israel; a kingdom upon the earth and this is the subject of much of the Old Testament. For example, consider Psalm 37:

> Those who hope in the Lord will inherit *the land* ... the righteous will inherit *the land* and dwell in it forever ... Wait for the Lord and keep his ways. He will exalt you to possess *the land.* (Psalm 37:9,11,22,29,34)

So Israel looked for a righteous kingdom in their land and the other nations would enjoy the surrounding area and would be blessed through Israel. This, also, is the subject of many passages. For example, consider the prophecy of Isaiah:

This is what Isaiah the son of Amoz saw concerning Judah and Jerusalem: In the last days the mountain of the Lord's temple will be established as chief among the mountains; it will be raised above the hills, and all nations will stream to it. Many people will come and say, "Come, let us go up to the mountain of the Lord, to the house of the God of Jacob. He will teach us his ways, so that we may walk in his paths."

The law will go out from Zion, the word of the Lord from Jerusalem. He will judge between the nations and will settle disputes for many peoples. They will beat their swords into ploughshares and their spears into pruning hooks. Nation will not take up sword against nation, nor will they train for war any more (Isaiah 2:1-4)

Arise, shine (Israel) for your light has come, and the glory of the Lord rises upon you. See, darkness covers the earth and thick darkness is over the people, but the Lord rises upon you and his glory appears over you. Nations will come to your light, and kings to the brightness of your dawn. (Isaiah 60:1-3)

This earthly kingdom, with Israel as centre and the nations coming to her for light and blessing, was the theme of the Old Testament, but it continued to be the message in the New. Both John the Baptist and the Lord Jesus Christ opened their ministry with the words, "Repent, for the kingdom of heaven is near," (Matthew 3:2; 4:17). There is a danger here that we will read the kingdom *of* heaven as the kingdom *in* heaven and not as the kingdom which originates in heaven but which is upon earth. That the Lord Jesus Christ was talking about the same kingdom upon earth as promised to Abraham and other Old Testament saints is indicated by two statements he made in the Sermon on the Mount.

> Blessed are the meek, for they will inherit the *earth* ... your kingdom come, your will be done on *earth* as it is in heaven. (Matthew 5:5; 6:10)

Just as the term "kingdom of heaven" is misunderstood so too are the Savior's words in John 18:26 when he said, "My kingdom is not of *(ek)* this world." Here He is saying that His kingdom does not originate in this world; it is not of *(ek)* this world; it is not *from* this world. "My kingdom is *from* another place," (John 18:36). It originates in heaven; it is of heaven; it is *from* heaven but it is upon earth. We are not denying that there is a heavenly aspect to the kingdom of God, which will be discussed shortly, but it is not the subject of the Old Testament, nor the subject of the Gospels, nor the subject of the Acts. This kingdom upon earth with *Israel as centre* was the subject of all writings during these different periods and it was for that reason the Lord sent out the twelve with the express command:

> Do not go among the Gentiles or enter any town of the Samaritans. Go rather to the lost sheep of Israel. (Matthew 10:5,6)

Some readers may be perplexed by these words from the Saviour of the world but they can be easily understood in the light of the Old Testament promises that the Gentiles were to receive their blessings through Israel. Thus, it was essential for Israel to get the message first and repent first. After that, a restored nation, they would take the message of the Messiah, His kingdom and eternal life to all other nations. That this was the Lord's intention is clear from Acts 1:8, where He told them that they were to be His witnesses in Jerusalem, in all Judea and Samaria and to the ends of the earth. Similarly, Luke 24:47 records that repentance and forgiveness of sins was to be preached in His name to all nations, beginning Jerusalem.

It is common knowledge that the offer extended to Israel in Matthew 10:7, and throughout the Lord's life on earth, was not accepted by that nation. They were responsible for crucifying their Messiah (Acts 5:31; 10:39) but His prayer for them was "Father, forgive them, for they do not know what they are doing," (Luke 23:34). Clearly this was answered for after Pentecost Peter once more offered to them the opportunity to repent, stating that if they did so then the times of refreshing and restoration would come from the Lord, (Acts 3:19-21). After an initial burst of response came the persecution and the nation did not listen to the ministry of the twelve, just as it had not listened to the ministry of the Lord Jesus Christ. What was the Lord to do then?

Acts 10 records something most unusual. Peter had the vision of the sheet containing various creatures which were unclean and the Holy Spirit spoke to him directly, telling him to go with the men sent by the Gentile Cornelius, (Acts 10:9-20). However when he met them he asked them, "Why have you come?" Later, on meeting Cornelius, he opened the conversation with, "May I ask why you have sent for me?" (Acts 10:29). These are hardly the words of a man desiring to spread the good news of the kingdom to the ends of the earth! Why did Peter ask such questions? After all, he had been told that repentance and forgiveness of sins was to be preached to all nations but he was told only to start at Jerusalem. With respect to what had been revealed to Peter up to this time, it was necessary for the nation of Israel first to respond, repent and be saved. After that their relatives, the Samaritans. Then the united and restored nation would take the message of their Messiah to the ends of the earth. However, that nation was not listening, thus there could be no message to the Gentile nations under the terms of the Old Testament. This explains Peter's reluctance to deal with Cornelius and his questions when they met. But why, if the nation was not responding, did the Holy Spirit guide Peter to the Gentile Cornelius?

Just after this event the Holy Spirit set apart Paul and Barnabas and sent them on various journeys which involved their travelling around the Mediterranean world, (Acts 13:2). They first visited the Jewish synagogues at Salamis and Pisidian Antioch, (Acts 13:5,15). However, they were often opposed in what they taught by members of the Jewish nation who refused to accept their testimony that Jesus was the Son of God, (Acts 13:6-12,45). When this happened they turned to the Gentiles in that area, (Acts 13:46). This was to be the pattern of their ministry throughout the Acts Period.

At Iconium they visited the Jewish synagogue but the Jews who refused to believe stirred up the Gentiles, (Acts 14:1,2). At Thessalonica there was a Jewish synagogue and Paul, as his custom was, went in and on three Sabbath days reasoned with them from the Scriptures, explaining and proving that the Christ had to suffer and rise from the dead. But the Jews rounded up some bad characters, formed a mob and started a riot in the city, (Acts 17:1-5). So Paul went to Berea but when the Jews of Thessalonica learned that Paul was preaching the word of God there, they went there too, agitating the crowds and stirring them up, (Acts 17:13).

So we see that Paul had two ministries during this period. One was to the people of Israel; "We had to speak the word of God to you first," (Acts 13:46). Throughout Paul's ministry during the book of Acts there can be little doubt that the Jew not only had an advantage, (Romans 3:1-2), but he also had first place, (Romans 1:16; 2:9,10; Acts 13:46). Also, it is clear that during this period what was on offer was exactly the same kingdom and promises that were proclaimed during the Old Testament and Gospel times.

> And now it is because of my hope in what God has promised our fathers, (Abraham, Isaac and Jacob), that I am on trial today. This is the promise our twelve tribes are hoping to see fulfilled as they earnestly serve God day and night. (Acts 26:6,7)

> For this reason I have asked to see you and talk with you. It is because of the hope of Israel that I am bound with this chain. (Acts 28:20)

What was the hope of Israel at that time? What was the promise made to the fathers; Abraham, Isaac and Jacob? It was for a kingdom upon the earth, with Jerusalem exalted and all Gentile nations coming to Israel for their blessings. This is the kingdom of the Old Testament, the Gospels, the Acts of the Apostles and the Epistles written during that time. Paul still hoped for a repentant and restored nation of Israel which would be a blessing to the surrounding Gentiles but that nation was not responding. Why then was Paul turning to the Gentiles?

On the Damascus Road Paul had been told that he would be a witness both of what he had seen and of what he would see, (Acts 26:16). We have considered some of the implications of that statement and it could be that something else was revealed to Paul after his vision on the Damascus Road, possibly when he was in Arabia. In Romans Paul wrote of something which had been a secret (mystery).

> I do not want you to be ignorant of this mystery (secret), brothers, so that you may not be conceited: Israel has experienced a hardening in part until the full number of Gentiles has come in. (Romans 11:25)

Israel of the Acts period had hardened their own hearts. Many had closed their own eyes to the Messiah and the result was the partial blindness of the nation. What did God do about this? He instructed Paul to turn to the Gentiles when any group of Jews rejected his ministry and the reason for doing that is given in Romans 11:11 – "Salvation has come to the Gentiles to make Israel envious."

This is not the reason for Gentile salvation today but it was during the Acts period. This action was designed in the hope that somehow the people of Israel might be aroused and saved. (Romans 11:14). Just as a wild olive branch could be grafted into a cultivated olive and stimulate it to bear more fruit, so the Gentiles of the Acts period were grafted into the Olive Tree of Israel and shared in that nation's blessings and promises, (Romans 11:17,18). This was the situation during the second half of the book of Acts and the only issue of debate was, would it work? Would Israel be stimulated to repent of their sin of rejecting the Lord Jesus Christ? Would they now accept Him as their Messiah? If they did, the times of restoration and refreshing would come as Peter had promised. (Acts 3:19-21).

Having these two ministries ensured that Paul would be a controversial character in his own day amongst his own people – and he still is today amongst Christians. His speeches in Acts and his earlier Epistles are often pondered over by believers who find them perplexing and enigmatic. One of the reasons for this is failure to appreciate that Paul had two ministries during the Acts period; one to the Jews, encouraging them to believe that the Lord Jesus Christ was their Messiah, the Son of God; the other was to the Gentiles, who were being saved and grafted into the Olive Tree of Israel in order to provoke that nation, hopefully, to repent. Although the basis for both ministries was the same and is also truth for today, some of what was taught was different in the two ministries and thus may not have any application to this age. However we will return to this subject later. We now have to consider the Acts of the Apostles. A reading of the closing chapters will make it clear that the nation of Israel was not provoked to repent.

In Rome Paul called the leaders of the Jews together and, from morning to evening, he explained and declared to them the kingdom of God and tried to convince them about Jesus from the law of Moses and from the Prophets, but they could not agree amongst themselves about what Paul had taught them, (Acts 28:17,23-25). Jerusalem had rejected the message. The Jewish synagogues of the many towns visited during the Acts period had rejected the message. Now Rome closed its doors also. What was to be done? It was no longer a question of hardening in part, or partial blindness. It was a case of complete hardness, blindness and deafness of the nation.

> They disagreed amongst themselves and began to leave after Paul had made this final statement: "The Holy

Spirit spoke the truth to your forefathers when he said through Isaiah the prophet: 'Go to this people and say, "You will be ever hearing but never understanding. You will be ever seeing but never perceiving." For this people's heart has become calloused; they hardly hear with their ears, and they have closed their eyes. Otherwise they might see with their eyes, hear with their ears, understand with their hearts and turn and I would heal them.' Therefore I want you to know that God's salvation has been sent to the Gentiles, and they will listen" For two whole years Paul stayed there in his own rented house and welcomed all who came to see him. Boldly and without hindrance he preached the kingdom of God and taught about the Lord Jesus Christ. (Acts 28:25-31)

Here we read the sixth and final New Testament quotation of the judgment foretold in Isaiah chapter 6, that the nation of Israel were to be blinded and deafened because they had hardened their hearts to God's message. But if that nation were now to be set aside by God, what message could Paul preach during those two years, and afterwards? If the Gentiles were to have been part of a kingdom upon the earth and were to have received their blessings through a restored Israel, what could Paul teach if that nation was blind, deaf and hard? To answer these questions we shall need to look at some of the Epistles Paul wrote during and after those two years in Rome.

6.

Paul's Third Ministry

6. PAUL'S THIRD MINISTRY

After the events described in Acts 28:25-28 Paul wrote seven epistles: Ephesians, Philippians, Colossians, 1 & 2 Timothy, Titus and Philemon. The basis of his ministry is, however, found in Ephesians and Colossians. We saw that Paul's ministry to the Gentiles during the Acts period was related to a mystery (secret), that Israel had experienced a hardening in part, (Romans 11:25). We will find that Paul's ministry after the end of Acts also revolves round this word mystery (secret).

> Surely you have heard about the administration of God's grace that was given to me for you, that is, the *mystery made known to me* by revelation, as I have already written briefly. In reading this, then, you will be able to understand my insight into *the mystery of Christ, which was not made known to men in other generations as it has now been revealed* by the Spirit to God's holy apostles and prophets. This mystery is that through the gospel the Gentiles are heirs together with Israel, members together in one body, and sharers together in the promise in Jesus Christ. (Ephesians 3:2-6)

> To preach to the Gentiles the unsearchable riches in Christ and to make plain to everyone the administration of *this mystery, which for ages past was kept hidden in God,* who created all things. His intent was that now, through the church, the manifold wisdom of God

should be made known to rulers and authorities in the heavenly realms. (Ephesians 3:8-10)

I have become its servant by the commission God gave me to present you the word of God in its fullness – *the mystery that has been kept hidden for ages and generations, but is now disclosed to the saints.* To them God has chosen to make known among the Gentiles the glorious riches of this mystery, which is Christ in you, the hope of glory. (Colossians 1:25-27)

What is this mystery or these mysteries that Paul mentions in these verses? What are these secrets which had not previously been known and were only then being revealed? The only way we can find out is to read the Epistles to the Ephesians and Colossians, and other relevant Scripture, and see if we can discover some new truths which have not previously been mentioned in the Scriptures. A diligent study of the seven Epistles written after Acts 28:25-28 will show them to be based solidly upon the truth of salvation by faith in Christ's completed work on Calvary's Cross. They also exalt the Lord Jesus Christ to the highest position of all and in these two respects they do not differ from the Gospel of John, the Epistle to the Romans or any of the earlier Epistles. However there is much that is new and different in them and we can select but two examples.

A phrase that is unique to Ephesians is *en tois epouraniois,* "in the heavenly realms" (NIV) or "in the heavenly places" (KJV). No longer is the believer told to look forward to a kingdom upon the earth. He is told that he has been raised and seated with Christ in the heavenly realms and it is there that the believer is to be given every spiritual blessing, (Ephesians 1:3; 2:6). If we have any doubts as to where these heavenly realms might be situated then they can be dispelled by reading Ephesians 1:19-21.

> That power is like the working of his mighty strength, which he exerted when he raised him from the dead and seated him at his own right hand in the heavenly realms, far above all rule and authority, power and dominion, and every title that can be given, not only in the present age but also in the one to come.

The heavenly realms are the regions to which Christ ascended to after His death and resurrection and there, not the earth, is the future home of believers since the setting aside of Israel at Acts 28:25-28. But after Israel lost its national privileges and promises, what was God to do with individual Jews and Gentiles who did believe in the Lord Jesus Christ? Ephesians tells us that he combined these two very different types of people into one new man.

> But now in Christ Jesus you who were far away have been brought near through the blood of Christ. For he himself is our peace, who has made the two one and has destroyed the barrier, the dividing wall, by abolishing in his flesh the law with its commandments and regulations. His purpose was to create in himself one new man out of the two, thus making peace, and in this one body to reconcile both of them to God through the cross, by which he put to death their hostility. (Ephesians 2:13-16)

In this new man there is no advantage for the Jew, no first place. The head of this new man is Christ Himself, (Ephesians 1:22-23), and the members of the body of this one new man are on a complete equality. In fact Ephesians 3:6 states that "This mystery is that through the gospel the Gentiles are heirs together with Israel, members together of one new body, and sharers together in the promise in Christ Jesus." Individual Jews and Gentiles who believed in Christ Jesus were equal heirs and equal partakers in a body of equal parts. This was certainly different from Deuteronomy 28:13 where Israel had been promised they were to be the head and not the tail. In a future kingdom upon this earth that will be their position, but not in this age.

As said above, the basis of the Epistles written after the events of Acts 28:25-28 is the same as those written before and it is profitable for us to remind ourselves of this basis.

> In him we have redemption through his blood, the forgiveness of sins, in accordance with the riches of God's grace. (Ephesians 1:17)

> For it is by grace you have been saved, through faith – and this is not of yourselves, it is the gift of God – not by works, so that no one can boast. (Ephesians 2:8,9)

The Gospel Period	The Acts Period		The Post Acts Period
	Acts 1-9	Acts 10 – 28:27	Acts 28:28 -
Jews only	Jews only	Jews first, then Gentiles to provoke Jews	Jews & Gentiles equal
Inheritance on earth	Inheritance on earth	Inheritance on earth	Inheritance in the heavenly realms
	Letters to Jews[1]	Letters to Jews and Gentiles: with the Jews first and the Gentiles grafted in.	Letters to Jews & Gentiles as equal members of one new man, the Body of Christ.
Matthew	Hebrews	Romans	Ephesians
Mark	James	1 Corinthians	Philippians
Luke	1 & 2 Peter	2 Corinthians	Colossians
John	1,2 & 3 John	Galatians	1 Timothy
	Jude	1 Thessalonians	2 Timothy
	Revelation	2 Thessalonians	Titus
			Philemon

[1] In this table we are not implying that all the letters written to Christian Jews were written during the early part of Acts. James probably was, and possibly Jude, but the others were more likely to have been written between Acts 10 and Acts 22.

Paul's Three Ministries 53

7.

A Comparison of the Three Ministries

7. A COMPARISON OF THE THREE MINISTRIES

Many readers of the Scriptures find the Epistles of Paul t difficult to understand and hard to reconcile the teaching within them. It certainly is an impossible task if we try to unify all that he wrote. If, however, we recognize that he had three different ministries then we will find that although there is much common ground, there are significant differences. We cannot deal with all the varying aspects of his three ministries but we shall consider the following examples.

(a) Circumcision

When writing to the Galatians Paul "that if you let yourselves be circumcised, Christ will be of no value to you at all. Again, I declare to every man who lets himself be circumcised that he is obliged to obey the whole law," (Galatians 5:2,3). We must first note that this was addressed to the Gentiles and this same issue came up for debate at the Jerusalem council for some men went down from Judea to Antioch and taught the brothers, "unless you are circumcised according to the custom of Moses, you cannot be saved." In addition some of the believers who belonged to the party of the Pharisees also taught, "the Gentiles must be circumcised and required to obey the Law of Moses," (Acts 15:1,2,5).

The apostles and elders met to discuss the questions and Peter asked why do they "try and test God by putting on the neck of the Gentiles a yoke that neither we nor the fathers have been able to bear," (Acts 15:10). The conclusion was voiced by James who said that they should not make it difficult for the Gentiles who were turning to God. The Gentiles did not have to be circumcised. Neither did they have to obey all the law. Only four commandments were given to them.

> It seemed good to the Holy Spirit and to us not to burden you with anything beyond the following requirements: You are to abstain food sacrificed to idols, from blood, from meat of strangled animals, and from sexual immorality. You will do well to avoid these things. (Acts 15:28,29)

Thus circumcision and obedience to the law was not part of Paul's message to the Gentiles of the Acts period – but what about the Christian Jew? Acts 16:1-3 record that Paul circumcised Timothy, whose father was a Gentile but whose mother was a Jewess. If she had been faithful to the Law of Moses she would have had him circumcised on the eighth day but evidently she did not. All the Jews in the area knew that Timothy's father was a Gentile and was likely to be uncircumcised and they would undoubtedly enquire. Thus Paul rightly circumcised Timothy, as he would any Jew. Thus it was rather unfair that Jews in Jerusalem had been told that Paul taught all the Jews who lived among the Gentiles to turn away from Moses, teaching them not to circumcise their children or live according to the Jewish customs, (Acts 21:21) – this passage is dealt with in detail in the next section). It would seem that Paul was misrepresented then as he can be nowadays, or what he taught the Gentiles was confused with what he taught the Jews. A mistake made in the first century A.D. and, possibly, in every century since.

During the Acts period Paul vigorously opposed any suggestion that the Gentiles should be circumcised but he supported obedience to the law of circumcision for the Jews. However once that people had lost their national privileges in Acts 28:25-28, things changed – not so much for the Gentiles but for the Jews. We read:

> For he is our peace, who has made the two one and has destroyed the barrier, the dividing wall of hostility, by abolishing *in his flesh* the law with its commandments and regulations. His purpose was to create in himself one new man out of the two, thus making peace, and in this one body to reconcile both of them to God *through the cross*, by which he put to death their hostility. (Ephesians 2:14-16). When you were dead in your sins and in the uncircumscision of your sinful nature, God made you alive with Christ. He forgave us all our sins, having cancelled the written code, with its regulations, that was against us and that stood opposed to us; he took it away, *nailing it to the cross.* (Colossians 2:13,14)

Thus for Israel the Lord abolished the law with its commandments and regulation. He cancelled the written code with its regulations. All this was achieved *by* or *through* the cross. However it did not come into operation *at* the cross. A reading of the Acts of the Apostles will show that the Jewish Christians still obeyed the law, but some readers may think that Ephesians and

Colossians teach that the Jews were freed from the commandments and regulations not only *by* the cross but also *at* the cross. This is, however, not the case. Many things were achieved *by* the death and resurrection of the Lord Jesus Christ but which were not put into practice then. For example: Hebrews 2:14 states that the Lord Jesus "Shared in their humanity so that *by* his death he might destroy him who holds the power of death – that is the devil." Yet, years later, Paul described Satan as the god of this age and the ruler of the kingdom of the air, (2 Corinthians 4:4; Ephesians 2:2). Not until Revelation 20 do we read of the future day when Satan is destroyed, following his release from the thousand-year captivity.

Again, we read in 2 Timothy 1:10 of "the appearing of our Savior, Christ Jesus, who has destroyed death and has brought life and immortality to life *by* the gospel." However we still have death with us and 1 Corinthians 15:26 states that "the last enemy to be destroyed is death" and this is destroyed in the lake of fire, just prior to the creation of the new heavens and earth, (Revelation 20:14).

The defeat of Satan, was assured *by* the cross but he was not vanquished *at* the cross. Death was destroyed *by* the cross but it did not cease *at* the cross. Similarly the commandments and regulations of the written code were abolished *by* the cross but their cancellation did not come in *at* the cross but came after the national blindness pronounced at Acts 28:25-28. Thus Paul could insist on circumcision for the Jews during the Acts period but afterwards he could write:

> In him (Christ) you were also circumcised, in the putting off of the sinful nature, not with a circumcision

done by the *hands of men but with the circumcision done by Christ.* (Colossians 2:11)

Thus once Israel had lost their national privileges, they were no longer under their nationalistic obligations which had been cancelled. Individual Jews were freed from their duty to circumcise their children and this was one great step towards making Jewish and Gentiles Christians one. The essential circumcision now is not the physical one done by the hands of men but the spiritual one done by Christ.

(b) The Law

As seen above, Paul objected to a Gentile being forced to obey the law, (Galatians 5:2,3). The council at Jerusalem imposed just four regulations upon the Christian Gentiles of the Acts period, (Acts 15:28, 29). However it should be noted that the Jews Christians, themselves, continued in their obedience and observations of the law. We can see this, for example, in the life of Paul himself.

> On the Sabbath day they entered the synagogue. (Acts 13:14)

> So he circumcised him because of the Jews. (Acts 16:3)

> On the Sabbath we went outside the city gate to the river, where we expected to find a place to pray. (Acts 16:13)

As his custom was, Paul went into the synagogue, and on three Sabbath days reasoned with them from the Scriptures. (Acts 17:2)

Every Sabbath he reasoned in the synagogue. (Acts 18:4)

Before he sailed, Paul had his hair cut off at Cenchrea because of a vow he had taken. (Acts 18:18; see Numbers 6:18)

We sailed from Phillipi after the feast of Unleavened Bread, (Acts 20:6)

Paul was in a hurry to reach Jerusalem, if possible, by the day of Pentecost, (Acts 20:16)

I did not realize that he was the high priest; for it is written: 'Do not speak evil about the ruler of your people.' (Acts 23:5; Exodus 22:27)

I was ceremonially clean when they found me in the temple courts. (Acts 24:18)

There can be no doubt that Paul was a Christian Jew and as such had great respect for the law. Consider this last example.

They said to Paul, "You see, brother, how many thousands of Jews have believed, and all of them are zealous for the law. They have been informed that you teach all the Jews who live among the Gentiles to turn away from Moses, telling them not to circumcise their children or live according to our customs. What shall we do? They will certainly hear that you have come, so do what we tell you. There are four men with us who have a vow. Take these men, join in their purification rites and pay their expenses, so that they can have their heads shaved. Then everybody will know there is no truth in these reports about you, but that you yourself are living in obedience to the law..." The next day Paul took the men and purified himself along with them. Then he went to the temple to give notice of the date when the days of purification would end and the offerings be made for each of them. (Acts 21:20-26; see also Numbers 6:1-18)

Bearing in mind that the above words were spoken by James, the leader of the Christian church in Jerusalem, we can see that there were significant differences between the Jewish Christians and the Gentile Christians of the Acts period and the words of Galatians 3:28, written during this time, are often misunderstood.

> There is neither Jew nor Greek, slave nor free, male nor female, for you are all one in Christ Jesus.

They most certainly were one in Christ Jesus and there was no difference between them with respect to sin and salvation but this verse does not teach complete equality and unanimity. There were differences between the Jewish and Gentile Christians during the Acts period, as can be seen from their differing obligations to the law in general and circumcision in particular. Also the Jew had first position, as we have read in Romans 1:16; 2:9,10; 3:1,2 and Acts 13:46. However after the close of the Acts period, the Lord Jesus Christ made the two, Jew and Gentile, one by destroying the barrier, the dividing wall of hostility, by abolishing the law with its commandments and ordinances, (Ephesians 2:14,15). The message is similar in Colossians which states that Christ "cancelled the written code, with its regulation, that was against us; he took it away, nailing it to the cross," (Colossians 2:14). Thus individual Jews were freed from their duty of obey the Law of Moses and this was another great step in making Jewish and Gentiles believers equal partakers in a body of equal parts.

(c) Food

We read earlier that the Gentiles of the Acts period were under no obligation to be circumcised or to obey the Mosaic Law. They had to abstain from sexual immorality and from "food sacrificed to idols, from drinking blood and from meat strangled"; i.e. animals killed by methods other than bleeding, which would mean that some of the blood stayed in the meat. Modern killing methods, such as the bolt to the brain, would not be acceptable under the principles of Acts 15:29 thus, if we take our teaching for today from this passage, we may have problems.

Throughout the Acts period, then, it appears that the Christian Gentiles had to observe these dietary regulations. However all this changed when the Law was abolished for Israel and when individual Jews and Gentiles were put on a complete equality. In Colossians 2:16 both groups were told that they should not let anyone judge them in what they ate or drank. They had been freed from such regulations and the manner in which an animal was killed was now irrelevant. A further great step in making these two into one new man, the body of Christ.

However Colossians 2:16 goes on to say much more. They were not to be judged with respect to religious festivals, new moon celebrations and Sabbath days. Can we imagine what such freedom from the law would mean for the Christian Jews of that time?

(d) The near return of Christ

In Acts 3:17 Peter told the people that it was through ignorance that they had crucified Christ and in saying that he was in complete harmony with the Lord's own words from the cross; "Father forgive them, for they do not know what they are doing," (Luke 23:34).

However Peter went on to urge the nation to repent, stating that if they did so, Christ would return.

> Now brothers, I know that you acted in ignorance, as did your leaders. But this is how God fulfilled what he had foretold through all the prophets, saying that his Christ would suffer. Repent, then, and turn to God, so that your sins may be wiped out, that times of refreshing may come from the Lord, and that he may send the Christ, who has been appointed for you – even Jesus. He must remain in heaven until the time comes for God to restore everything, as he promised long ago through his holy prophets. (Acts 3:17-21)

Everything would be restored; the times of refreshing would come; their sins would be wiped out ... He would send the Christ – even Jesus ... if only they repented. This was Peter's message and not only his, but all the apostles taught the possibility of Christ's return during the Acts period. For example:

- Peter wrote: "the end of all things is near." (1 Peter 4:7)

- James wrote: "Be patient, then, brothers, until the Lord's coming. See how the farmer waits for the land to yield its valuable crop and how patient he is for the autumn and spring rains. You too, be patient and stand firm, because the Lord's coming is near. Don't grumble against each other, or you will be judged. The Judge is standing at the door!" (James 5:7-9)

- John wrote: "Dear children, this is the last hour, and as you have heard that the antichrist is coming, even now many antichrists have come. This is how we know it is the last hour." (1 John 2:18)

- John again: "The revelation of Jesus Christ, which God gave to him to show his servants what must soon take place ... Blessed is the one who reads the words of this prophecy, and blessed are those who hear it and take to heart what is written in it, because the time is near ... Here I am, I stand at the door and knock ... The Lord, the God of the spirits of the prophets, sent his angel to show his servants the things that must soon take place. 'Behold, I am coming soon!' ... Do not seal up the words of the prophecy of this book, because the time is near ... 'Behold I am coming soon!' ... He who testifies to these things says, 'Yes, I am coming soon.'" (Revelation 1:1,3; 3:20; 22:6,7,10,12,20)

- Jude quoted Enoch who wrote: "See, the Lord is coming with thousands upon thousands of his holy ones to judge everyone." (Jude 14,15)

Paul also taught this great truth during the Acts period and showed that all the Christian Jews were still hoping for a national repentance on the part of Israel, which would usher in the return of the Lord and the establishment of the kingdom upon earth. Before Agrippa Paul said: "And now it is because of my hope in what God promised our fathers that I am on trial today. This is the promise our *twelve tribes are hoping to see fulfilled* as they earnestly serve God day and night," (Acts 26:6,7). He also wrote much about the nearness of the return of Christ, and the difficult times which would precede it, in a number of his earlier Epistles.

> Hebrews 10:25,37: - "Let us not give up meeting together, as some are in the habit of doing, but let us encourage one another – and all the more as you see the Day approaching … For in just a very little while, 'He who is coming will come and will not delay.'"

> Romans 13:12: - "The night is nearly over; the day is almost here. So let us put aside the deeds of darkness and put on the armour of light."

> 1 Thessalonians 1:9,10: - "They tell how you turned to God from idols to serve the living and true God, and to wait for his Son from heaven."

> 1 Corinthians 1:7: - "Therefore you do not lack in any spiritual gift as you eagerly wait for our Lord Jesus Christ to be revealed."

1 Corinthians 7:26-29: - "Because of the present crisis, I think it is good for you to remain as you are. Are you married? Do not seek a divorce. Are you unmarried? Do not look for a wife. But if you do marry, you have not sinned; and if a virgin marries, she has not sinned. But those who marry will face many troubles in this life, and I want to spare you. What I mean, brothers, is that the time is short."

From 1 Thessalonians 4:15,17 and 1 Corinthians 15:51,52 it is clear that Paul expected the return of Christ during his lifetime and this is why he was advising people not to get married. If Israel did respond then before the Lord Jesus did return the nation would have to go through the great and terrible day of the Lord, the great tribulation. Speaking of this time, the Lord Jesus said:

Then let those who are in Judea flee to the mountains … how dreadful it will be in those days for pregnant women and nursing mothers! Pray that your flight will not take place in the winter or on the Sabbath. For then there will be great distress, unequalled from the beginning of the world until now. (Matthew 24:16-21)

However we know that the nation did not respond. They hardened themselves and became both blind and deaf, (Acts 28:25-28). As a result Israel lost its privileges and promises, including the offer that Christ would return at that time and restore all things to them if they repented. Thus we do not find any such statements about the nearness of Christ's return, or of it being the last hour, in the Epistles written after Acts 28:25-28. In fact the word *parousia*, which means "coming" or presence" and which is used frequently of Christ's second coming in the gospels and earlier Epistles, is never used of the Lord in any of the later Epistles. There is no mention of the Lord's *parousia* (coming) in Ephesians, Philippians, Colossians, 1 and 2 Timothy, Titus and Philemon.

Further, it is significant that Paul changed his advice in his later Epistles, when the return of Christ was no long imminent. Life could not continue as normal and Paul's advice to the young widows was:

> So I counsel younger widows to marry, to have children, to manage their homes and to give the enemy no opportunity for slander. (1 Timothy 5:14)

(e) Healing

In Acts 2:22 we read that Jesus of Nazareth was a man accredited to Israel by miracles, wonders and signs, which God did through Him among that nation. These were the miracles the prophets said the Messiah would do. Those miracles were His credentials.

Similarly the salvation in Christ, which was announced by the apostles during the Acts period, needed some credentials if the Jewish nation were to listen to those who preached it. God testified of the authenticity of the message and those who proclaimed it with wonders, various miracles and gifts of the Holy Spirit, (Hebrews 2:4). We can see the effect of such a miracle upon the people of Israel when Peter and James healed the man at the Beautiful Gate. The people were astonished and came to listen to what Peter had to say.

If Paul was to have a ministry to the people of Israel then it was essential that he should also be accredited by the same signs and this we see during the Acts of the Apostles. He performed many miracles, including the following.

> So Paul and Barnabas spent considerable time there, speaking boldly for the Lord, *who confirmed the message of his grace by enabling them to do miraculous signs and wonders.* (Acts 14:3)

> In Lystra there sat a man crippled in his feet, who was lame from birth and had never walked. He listened to Paul as he was speaking. Paul looked directly at him, saw he had faith to be healed and called out, "Stand up on your feet!" At that, the man jumped up and began to walk. (Acts 14:8-10)

> God did extraordinary miracles through Paul. Handkerchiefs and aprons that had touched him were taken to the sick and their illnesses were cured and the evil spirits left them. (Acts 19:11,12)

> Seated in a window was a young man named Eutychus, who was sinking into a deep sleep as Paul talked on and on. When he was sound asleep, he fell to the ground from the third story and was picked up dead. Paul went down, threw himself on the young man and put his arms around him. "Don't be alarmed," he said. "He's alive!" Then he went upstairs again and broke bread and ate. After talking until daylight, he left. The people took the young man home alive and were greatly comforted. (Acts 20:9-12)

Publius' father was sick in bed, suffering from fever and dysentery. Paul went to see him and, after prayer, placed his hands on him and healed him. When this had happened, the rest of the sick on the island came and were cured. (Acts 28:8,9)

In Acts we see the healing of both Jews and Gentiles, who were sharing in the blessings as a wild olive which had been grafted into a cultivated one and which partook of its nourishing sap, (Romans 11:17). However, once the nation had hardened its heart and become blind and deaf, it lost its national privileges and God was no longer witnessing to it as a nation. Thus such miraculous credentials were no longer needed and it is significant that in the Epistles written after Acts 28:25-28 not only is there no record of an instant healing but there are, in fact, three clear testimonies of Paul's inability to heal.

In 2 Timothy 4:20 Paul simply states that he had left Trophimus sick in Miletus. Earlier, in Acts 28:8-9, Paul left no one unhealed on Malta.

Then in 1 Timothy 5:23 Paul gives Timothy the following advice: "Stop drinking only water, and use a little wine because of your stomach and your frequent infirmities." Again, earlier, a handkerchief or apron sent from Paul cured the sick (Acts 19:11,12) but now Paul sent only advice.

Lastly, we read in Philippians 2:25-28:

> But I think it necessary to send back to you Epaphroditus, my brother, fellow-worker and fellow

soldier, who is also your messenger, whom you sent to take care of my needs. For he longs for all of you and is distressed because you heard he was ill. Indeed he was ill, and almost died. But God had mercy on him, and not on him only but also on me, to spare me sorrow upon sorrow. Therefore I am all the more eager to send him, so that when you see him again you may be glad and I may have less anxiety.

If Paul still possessed the gift of immediate and instant healing he would not have had any sorrow, let alone sorrow upon sorrow. No doubt Paul prayed for his fellow-worker and when Epaphroditus recovered, Paul gave the glory and his thanks to God. We can do the same and it will save us lots of scriptural problems if we appreciate that we are Gentiles who live in accordance with Paul's later ministry rather than in accordance with his earlier ones.

8.
Conclusion

8. CONCLUSION

When we study the Bible not only is it essential for us to realize that all Scripture is God-breathed but we must also be aware that all Scripture is useful for teaching, rebuking, correcting and training in righteousness, (2 Timothy 3:16). We can learn much about God and mankind in general by an understanding of the events in the Old Testament, as 1 Corinthians 10:6 makes clear. However, if we insist that all Scripture has the same message to every people at every time and on every aspect of God's plan, then we will be doing both God and His Word a dis-service. Certainly there are exhibitions of God's love and grace, His patience and longsuffering, His righteousness and justice throughout the Scriptures, from Genesis to Revelation. So, also is man's sinfulness and selfishness, and his despair at death, from which he cannot escape without the gift of God's righteousness, which is freely given to those who believe. "Without the shedding of blood there is no remission for sin" underlines the way God has provided for man's salvation and the need for that one great sacrifice for sin does not alter. As we have seen, it is common to all three ministries of the apostle Paul.

Neither does God modify the moral standards He sets for men. Whether we read the Law of Moses, the Sermon on the Mount, James' Epistle to the dispersion of Israel, Paul's words to the Corinthians during the Acts period or his exhortations to the Ephesians and Colossians – in all these the practical truths and the moral messages are the same. But as we have seen, during the Acts period God was dealing with two very different groups of people; Jews, who had been brought up on their Scriptures and who had a great knowledge of God, and Gentiles, who had a pagan background with its teachings of many gods. To send exactly the same message to both and to expect exactly the same response from two such differing groups would have been unjust. The foundation for both was the same, the Lord Jesus Christ, but the buildings erected on that foundation had, understandably, some differences and to recognize these and understand them will give us greater confidence in the Scriptures and will increase our faith in the all wise God.

Similarly we saw that there were further differences when Israel lost its national privileges at the end of the book of Acts. Its responsibilities and obligations to the Law were also withdrawn and God placed individual Christian Jews and individual Christian Gentiles on a complete equality. They became equal heirs, equal sharers, equal members of a body of equal parts of which Christ was and still is, the Head. The promise of eternal life in an earthly kingdom, of which Israel was to be the centre and through whom the Gentiles were to receive their blessings, was the hope of the Old Testament, the Gospels, the Acts and the Epistles written during that time – and God will, one day, fulfill that hope. However, after the blinding, deafening and hardening of national Israel God revealed a new hope, one in the heavenly realms (places). Now the believer is raised and seated with the ascended Christ.

****

In this study we have tried to heed the words of Miles Coverdale who stated that it would greatly help us to understand the Scriptures if we took into account:

Not only what is written but of whom it is written, and to whom, with what words and at what time, where, to what intent and with what circumstances, considering what goes before and what comes after[2].

In other words, let us recognize that the Lord, in His wisdom, has given some different instructions to different people at different times. He used His servant Paul and gave him three different ministries. The basic message about sin and salvation and the person of the Lord Jesus Christ did not change. However other parts were altered. To recognize this makes the Scriptures authoritative and alive. It makes them the Word of God. To acknowledge such changes makes us think about what God is doing and why he is doing it. It makes us consider His eternal purpose, (Ephesians 3:11), and realize that He has a plan for the earth as well as one for the heavens and, one day, He will restore Israel to fulfill His goal for the earth. That, however, will be after He has fulfilled his heavenly one with the church which is His body, and which believing Jews and Gentiles have a complete equality and of which Christ is the Head.

---

[2] For a full application of this life see *Approaching the Bible* by Michael Penny, published by The Open Bible Trust. Details on page 74.

More on Paul

Paul: A Missionary of Genius
By Michael Penny

"One good reason why Christianity was triumphant was that it found in Saul of Tarsus, later St. Paul, a missionary of genius ... Though himself a Jew, Paul took this new and startling religion out of Judaism into the world of the Gentiles," wrote the novelist J B Priestley.

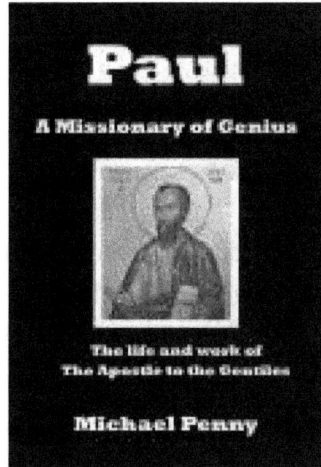

Paul

A Missionary of Genius

The life and work of
The Apostle to the Gentiles

Michael Penny

But what do we know about this man Saul, who became Paul? This book deals with the life and work of the only person the New Testament calls "The Apostle to the Gentiles."

As well as covering all his life (from Tarsus, to Jerusalem, to Antioch and eventually on to Rome), this book also covers all his teaching from his two-fold commission in Acts (to go to the Gentiles as well as Jews) to his final commission relating to the Body of Christ, where there is neither Jew nor Gentile.

- **This book will give Christians not only a better understanding of Paul and his writing, but also a better appreciation of the whole New Testament.**

About the Author

Michael Penny was born in Ebbw Vale, Gwent, Wales in 1943. He read Mathematics at the University of Reading, before teaching for twelve years and becoming the Director of Mathematics and Business Studies at Queen Mary's College Basingstoke in Hampshire, England. In 1978 he entered Christian publishing, and in 1984 became the administrator of the Open Bible Trust.

He held this position for seven years, before moving to the USA and becoming pastor of Grace Church in New Berlin, Wisconsin. He returned to Britain in 1999, and is at present the Administrator and Editor of The Open Bible Trust.

From 2010 to 2018 he was Chairman of Churches Together in Reading, where he speaks in a number of churches, and was a chaplain at reading College and on the advisory committee to Reading University Christian Union..

He lives near Reading with his wife and has appeared on BBC Radio Berkshire and Premier Radio a number of times. He has made several speaking tours of America, Canada, Australia, New Zealand and the Netherlands, as well as ones to South Africa and the Philippines. Some of his writings have been translated into Russian.

As well as editing and writing articles for *Search* magazine and many Bible study booklets, he has also written several major books including: *The Manual on the Gospel of John; 40 Problem Passages; Approaching the Bible; Galatians - Interpretation and Application; The Miracles of the Apostles; Introducing God's Word* (with Carol Brown and Lynn Mrotek); *Introducing God's Plan* (with Sylvia Penny).

Recent books are *The Bible! Myth or Message?*, *The Balanced Christian Life* (based on Ephesians, and is designed for use with Lent Studies and House Group Bible Studies).

He has written two books with W M Henry

- *Following Philippians*, which is ideal for Post-Alpha groups

- *The Will of God: Past and Present.*

His latest books are:

- *Joel's Prophecy: Past and Future*

- *James; His Life and Letter*

- *Paul: A Missionary of Genius*

Details of these books, and other writings, can be seen at

www.obt.org.uk

Further Reading

Approaching the Bible

Michael Penny

In easy to understand steps, this book sets out to encourage and stimulate Christians to approach the Bible for themselves. With many interesting examples, Michael Penny provides the rational for the view that before we try to *apply* any passage in the Bible to ourselves, we should discover first what it meant to those to whom its words were initially addressed. The book advocates that this is best done by considering the passage under the following headings:

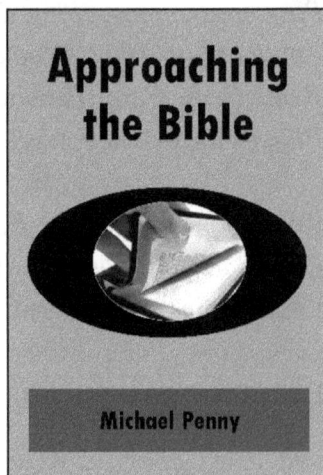

1) **W**ho said or wrote it;
2) to **W**hom was it said or written, or concerning **W**hom was it said or written;
3) **W**here it was said or written, or concerning **W**here was it said or written;
4) **W**hat was said or written;
5) **W**hen was it said or written, or concerning **W**hen was it said or written;
6) **W**hy was it said or written.

Applying these six **"W"** rules puts the passage into its proper context and gives us the right perspective on it. Only after doing this can we determine:

7) **W**hether the passage applies to our situation and what the correct application is.

It is the *consistent* use of these **Seven Ws** which helps us discover the right and relevant application of any passage to our lives.

Further details on

www.obt.org.uk

Free Magazine:

Michael Penny is editor of *Search* magazine

For a free sample of
the Open Bible Trust's magazine Search,
please visit

www.obt.org.uk/search

or email

admin@obt.org.uk

About this Book

Paul's Three Ministries

The Apostle Paul has often been considered a controversial character. Some writers have suggested that on certain doctrine she changed his mind. Others have claimed that as Paul grew older, he developed his theology and changed his some of his teachings.

In this publication Michael Penny shows that it was God who gave him different things to say and who changed Paul's ministry. For example, God told Ananias that Paul would have two very different and distinct ministries. He said

"This man is my chosen vessel to carry my name before *the Gentiles* and their kings and before *the people of* Israel." (Acts 9:19)

This publication considers the similarities and differences between those two ministries, and explains why they differed.

It also compares those earlier two ministries with a third, a later one which God gave him; one in which distinctions between Jews and Gentiles were abolished.

www.ingramcontent.com/pod-product-compliance
Lightning Source LLC
Chambersburg PA
CBHW070550030426
42337CB00016B/2434